TAOS PUEBLO

Rio Nuevo Publishers®
P.O. Box 5250, Tucson, Arizona 85703-0250
(520) 623-9558, www.rionuevo.com

Front cover, page 43: Denver Public Library, Western History Department, No. F41208. Back cover and pages
1, 51: Denver Public Library, Western History Department, No. F6023. Pages 3, 21: Arizona State Museum,
University of Arizona, No. 33771. Page 4: Museum of New Mexico, No. 42967. Pages 5, 54: Denver Public
Library, Western History Department, No. P221. Page 8: Museum of New Mexico, No. 16096. Page 13:
Posthumous digital reproduction from original negative, Edward Weston Archive, Center for Creative
Photography, © 1981 Arizona Board of Regents. Page 15: Museum of NewMexico, No. 4500. Page 17:
Museum of New Mexico, No. 54091. Page 18: Museum of New Mexico, No. 4594. Pages 24-25: Museum of
New Mexico, No. 31270. Page 28: Denver Public Library, Western History Department, No. P529. Page 31:
Arizona State Museum, University of Arizona, No. 33770. Page 34: Museum of New Mexico, No. 43155. Page
36: Museum of New Mexico, No. 86263. Page 40: Museum of New Mexico, No. 42978. Page 46: Arizona State
Museum, University of Arizona, No. 39908. Pages 58-59, endsheets: Colorado Historical Society, No. F34,074.

Cover and interior design by Karen Schober, Seattle, Washington

Library of Congress Cataloging-in-Publication Data

Bodine, John J.
Taos Pueblo : a walk through time / John J. Bodine.
    p. cm. — (Look West series)
Originally published: Santa Fe, N.M. : Lightning Tree, c1977.
ISBN-13: 978-1-887896-95-5 (hardcover)
ISBN-10: 1-887896-95-3 (hardcover)
1. Taos Pueblo (N.M.) 2. Taos Indians. I. Title. II. Series.
E99.T2B63 2006
917.89'53—dc22
                            2006017843
Printed in Korea.

10 9 8 7 6 5 4 3 2 1

TAOS PUEBLO

A WALK THROUGH TIME

John J. Bodine

LOOK WEST
SERIES

RIO NUEVO PUBLISHERS
TUCSON, ARIZONA

‖ TO THE VISITOR ‖

THE PEOPLE OF TAOS PUEBLO WELCOME
YOU TO THEIR ANCIENT HOME. APPROXIMATELY 1,500
TAOS ARE LIVING HERE TODAY, AND THROUGH THEIR HOSPITALITY
YOU ARE ABLE TO SEE ONE OF THE MOST UNUSUAL SETTLEMENTS
IN THE UNITED SSTATES, IF NOT IN THE WORLD.
THEY ONLY ASK THAT YOU OBSERVE A FEW SIMPLE RULES,
WHICH ARE NECESSARY TO PROTECT THEIR PRIVACY
AND THE INTEGRITY OF THEIR COMMUNITY.

Photography is permitted only by permission and payment of a modest fee as you enter the Pueblo. No photographs are permitted during the ceremonials. Cameras and tape recorders should be left

LEFT: *North Pueblo, Taos Pueblo, ca. 1912,* by Jesse L. Nusbaum.

— 5 —

MAP OF TAOS PUEBLO

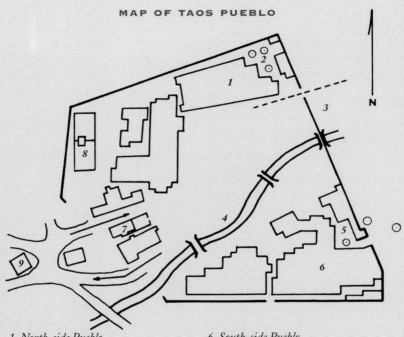

1 North-side Pueblo
2 North-side Kivas
3 Pueblo Wall
4 River
5 South-side Kivas

6 South-side Pueblo
7 St. Jerome (San Geronimo) Mission
8 Ruined Church and Cemetery
9 Pueblo Government Offices and
   Public Restrooms

locked in your car during those times. Photographs of individuals and their activities may be taken if you secure the permission of those involved.

No home should be entered unless you are specifically invited. Moreover, you will notice "restricted" signs and barricades (usually sawhorses) set up at various places around the village. You are not allowed to go beyond these. Climbing ladders and going onto roofs is as offensive to the owners of these homes as it would be if strangers came to your property and did the same. Believe it or not, many visitors have done it!

A receptacle for trash is provided in the center of the village near the river. Please do not throw anything into the river as this is a primary source for drinking and cooking water.

We sincerely hope that you enjoy your visit and that this guide will help you understand what you see and experience. The book is divided into two parts. The first is a brief description of various features of the Pueblo that are of special interest. It is organized in terms of a walking tour that will take you to the most important places in the village. The second part (starting on page 27) can be read at leisure. It will provide answers to questions you may have about the lives of the Taos people and the unusual culture they have preserved for so many centuries.

‖ A WALKING TOUR OF TAOS PUEBLO ‖

Most probably you have entered the Pueblo and parked on the north side of the plaza—the open space between the house clusters. If you turn and face the north-side houses you will see the sight that is justly famous around the world. It is relatively unchanged since the men of Coronado's expedition first saw it in 1540.

In 1992, the old village of Taos Pueblo was designated a World Heritage Site by the World Heritage Foundation under the auspices of the United Nations. Taos Pueblo thus joins such famous places as the Taj Mahal, the Great Wall of China, the Pyramids of Egypt, and Vatican City, among others. You are indeed looking at a world-recognized historical site.

THE MOUNTAINS

Rising majestically behind the Pueblo are the peaks of the Sangre de Cristo Mountains. The early Spanish explorers named them the "Blood of Christ" when they saw them bathed a vibrant red during a spectacular sunset. The most prominent peak is called simply Taos Mountain. It rises 12,282 feet above sea level and is sacred to the

Taos Pueblo, 1880, by John K. Hillers.

Taos people. Behind Taos Mountain but not visible from the valley floor is Wheeler Peak, which at 13,151 feet is the highest point in the state of New Mexico. The Taos Indians have used the mountainous area behind the Pueblo for hunting, fishing, firewood, and plant life, as well as for ceremonial purposes, since they first settled close to the present Pueblo sometime in the fourteenth century.

THE NORTH-SIDE PUEBLO

Walk toward the architectural triumph that is said to be one of the most photographed and painted buildings in the New World. This and the south-side Pueblo were built about AD 1350. At a height of five stories, the north-side Pueblo of Taos is the largest multistoried Pueblo structure still existent and continuously inhabited. It is made entirely of adobe and the walls are frequently several feet thick. The roofs of each story were made by placing large timbers, called *vigas* (VEE-gahs), on the adobe walls. Smaller pieces of wood were placed side by side across the vigas to form the ceiling of the room below. The whole was then covered with adobe to seal the roof.

A primary reason for building the Pueblo several stories high was defense. Today you see that windows and doors have been cut

In front of the north-side Pueblo are several drying racks for jerked meat, corn, and other crops. It is not advisable to climb on

Ovens, Taos Pueblo, 1933, by Edward Weston.

them, as they are seldom used anymore and may not be sound. Behind the buildings are many racks, similar in construction, used for drying and storing hay for livestock. At times corn and plums for winter use are also dried on the roofs of the Pueblo.

If you are facing the north-side Pueblo, turn right and walk down to the low adobe wall and the last of the three bridges that span the river.

THE KIVAS *(KEE-VAHS)*

At the far or east end of the north-side Pueblo, close up among the final cluster of houses, you will notice tall ladder poles projecting out of fence-like enclosures. These mark the entrances to the three kivas on the north side. A kiva is a sacred ceremonial chamber used primarily by the men for religious rituals. At Taos, unlike certain other pueblos, all six kivas are subterranean. Three are here on the north side, one is directly opposite these on the south side, and two more are located outside the village wall on the south. These large underground rooms are as sacred to the Taos as the inner city of Mecca is to the Moslems or the altar at St. Peter's is to Catholics. It is absolutely forbidden for a non-Taos, even another Indian, to enter these ceremonial chambers. Barricades have been erected to remind you not to approach them.

A south-side kiva with ladder for descent, Taos Pueblo, ca. 1910, by George L. Beam.

THE PUEBLO WALL

If you are now at the east end of the village, you will see a rather low adobe wall. The wall completely encloses the village, except for the area through which you entered. It was once much higher, for protection against marauding tribes. In 1776, when the Declaration of Independence was being written on the East Coast of the continent, this wall protected the Indians and a few Spanish settlers, who had moved into the Pueblo, from raids by the Comanches. At that time, four large watchtowers, strategically placed at the corners of the Pueblo, allowed the inhabitants to observe the movements of possible enemies. There was also a massive gate, near where you entered the village, to permit the passage of people and animals. Livestock were brought into corrals in the village at night to protect them from the Comanches or other raiders. Today the wall is maintained as a symbol of the village boundaries.

RIO PUEBLO DE TAOS, OR THE RIVER

As mentioned before, the sparkling water from this river is the primary source for drinking and cooking water for the residents of the village proper. Numerous wells have been dug at homesites outside the village to serve the many who live some distance from the river. You may well see women or children carrying water in buckets back

Rio Pueblo de Taos, 1881, by William Henry Jackson.

to their homes. Formerly the women used pottery jars balanced on their heads. Horses and other livestock are always watered below the last of the three bridges that span the creek. The river never freezes completely, although heavy ice will sometimes form in winter. But the river moves so swiftly that the ice can be broken to obtain the water flowing beneath.

South-Side Pueblo, Taos Pueblo, ca. 1885, by Dana P. Chase.

The source of this river is the sacred Blue Lake of the Taos, high in the mountains between Taos Mountain and Mt. Wheeler. This wilderness area was incorporated into the Carson National Forest in 1906 by order of President Theodore Roosevelt. The Taos Indians fought for sixty-four years for the return of these sacred lands to their reservation. In 1970 by an act of Congress and the signature of the president, 48,000 acres of mountain lands including Blue Lake were returned to the Taos. It marked the first time in the long history of U.S.-Indian relations that land illegally seized by the government was returned to an Indian tribe on the basis of freedom of religious worship.

THE SOUTH-SIDE PUEBLO

If you cross the river by means of the nearest bridge, you can view the south-side Pueblo of Taos more easily. Much that has been said of the north side applies to this cluster of homes, except that on the south the building rises only four stories. You have surely noticed signs on either side advertising arts and crafts. You are welcome to enter these homes converted into shops, to see the handicrafts. The Taos manufacture an unusual form of pottery made of micaceous clay in which tiny flecks of mica gleam in the light. Often the pots are not sufficiently fired to hold water and should not be used for cooking unless the potter tells you that she has hard-fired the vessel. The Taos, great hunters as well as farmers, are more famous for their work with skins. They still make durable moccasins and the whitened doeskin boots of the women, as well as excellent drums.

While on the south side, look beyond the Pueblo buildings to the hill that rises on the south. Just in front of the hill is the Bureau of Indian Affairs Day School complex for children in grades 1–6.

THE MISSION OF ST. JEROME

If you proceed along the south-side houses and recross the river at the last bridge, you will be close to the Catholic Mission of St. Jerome, or San Geronimo. He is the patron saint of the Pueblo. This church was built after the previous one was destroyed in the Rebellion of 1847. You are welcome to go in and take a look at the objects of veneration, many of them very old, which the Taos have preserved for so long in their practice of Catholicism. The majority of the Indians are Catholics. A few have converted to Protestantism, principally to the Baptist Church. Actually, three religions are represented at Taos: Christianity, the aboriginal religion, and the Native

Mission of St. Jerome, Taos Pueblo, ca. 1930, by Forman Hanna.

American Church, often called the peyote religion. All three are strongly practiced, although not all Taos people belong to each. But it is not inconsistent in their system for a person to worship in three ways, since each religion offers different messages and different tenets of faith.

THE RUINED CHURCH AND CEMETERY

After leaving the Mission of St. Jerome, turn left sharply and walk down the road on which you entered the village. When you come to the main intersection at the entrance, look at the open space to your right and you will see the ruined adobe bell tower of the "old church," which was destroyed in the 1847 Rebellion. You may walk up to the ruins and the cemetery which they enclose. They are eloquent testaments of a dramatic event still remembered by the Pueblo.

In 1847 the United States took possession of what is now New Mexico as a result of the war with Mexico. Many of the Spanish-speaking people in Taos Valley remained loyal to the Mexican cause and enlisted the support of some of the Taos Indians against the Americans. In the violent encounter that followed, the first U.S. territorial governor of New Mexico, Charles Bent, was scalped and killed. (You may visit his home, where this happened, on Bent Street in the nearby town of Taos.) In retaliation, the U.S. Army came up from Santa Fe to Taos Pueblo. The Indians took refuge and fought valiantly in this old church, but they were no match for the cannons of the Army. One hundred fifty Indians were killed in the prolonged and bloody battle, and later a number were hanged for their part in the insurrection.

It was customary in the past to bury the dead in the courtyards of Catholic churches and at times even under the floor inside the church itself. This is rarely done elsewhere today, but the Taos have retained the custom of burying their dead between the walls of their ruined church. Now many generations of Taos have been buried here. No one knows where the burial ground of the Taos was prior to the coming of the Spanish missionaries. Indeed, it is possible that another form of disposal of the deceased was used, such as cremation—a method employed by other tribes in pre-European times. Nevertheless, interment in the ground is and has been the Taos custom since the early 1600s.

Some persons have been buried in coffins recently, but this is not the traditional Indian way. Taos who are still buried in the old

OVERLEAF: Ruins of the old mission are prominent twelve years after the Rebellion of 1847 in this unattributed artist's sketch.

way are dressed in their finest and carefully wrapped in blankets. The body is then lowered by rope into the grave and a simple wooden cross erected. After a period of time, the body decays and returns to the earth, and the cross deteriorates. The plot can them be reused. In this fashion additional generations have been accommodated in the cemetery. It would be considered extremely impolite for you to enter the cemetery and destructive to climb or sit on the old walls.

As you drive out the road leading to the town of Taos, you come to Oo-oonah, the Taos Indian Children's Art Center, on your right. The Center was conceived by the late Stan Aiello, who served as art instructor at the Pueblo Day School. Recognizing the unusual talent of many of the Pueblo children, Mr. Aiello worked diligently for the establishment of this center. Proceeds from the sale of the children's art go to the maintenance of the Center, and a percentage is given to the child whose art is sold.

You have now seen the highlights of the tour of Taos Pueblo. Much more can be said about this Pueblo and its inhabitants. Many of your questions will be answered in the second part of the book.

‖ THE PUEBLO, PAST AND PRESENT ‖

While a great deal has been written about Taos Indians and the Pueblo particularly, there still remains a good deal of misunderstanding about this famous place and the lives of its people. Hopefully in the material that follows, a few of these errors are corrected and the questions that occur to most visitors to Taos are answered.

THE NAME TAOS AND THE TAOS LANGUAGE

The word *Taos* is unusual, and many have speculated on its origin and meaning. Romantic writers who see in Taos culture a profound philosophy and way of life have wondered if Taos is not in some way related to the ancient Chinese religion, Taoism. It is not. Indeed, it is not even pronounced in the same way. There is no reliable evidence to link the Taos Indians with the Chinese. The languages of the two peoples are not related in any way, and one must stretch very hard to find even broad parallels with certain cultural beliefs. Taos is a one-syllable word pronounced by most in the same way as the English word "house." Many visitors will mispronounce it "TAY-os."

As to its origin, it seems conclusive that the word has roots in the languages of some of the other Pueblo Indians of New Mexico—

those who speak Tanoan languages and live along the Rio Grande River from Taos down to Isleta, just south of Albuquerque. The Spanish explorers first came to the Rio Grande south of Taos. In trying to communicate with the Indians there and asking them about the villages to the north, they were given a term that meant "to the north." It is also a term that can be found in the Taos language and means, in addition to direction, "to or toward the village." The term was roughly "tao." The Spanish were in the habit of adding an "s" to nouns to form the plural—so the result was Taos. It has been in use ever since 1598. Unfortunately for the romantics, there is nothing mysterious about it.

There is also a good deal of misunderstanding about the Taos language. Again, attempts have been made to link the speech of the Taos Indians with the Chinese. Part of this is due to the fact that the Taos language is partially tonal and Chinese is tonal. English and other European languages are not, but speakers of those languages hear what they describe as a "singsong" or musical quality to tonal speech. Hence, there must be some connection. The Taos language is no more related to Chinese than English is. There are many tonal

Taos Pueblo Indian, ca. 1908–1925, by H. S. Poley.

languages in the world. For example, Navajo is tonal and so are many of the languages in Central Africa, but you never hear anyone suggesting they are related to Taos.

Taos is a Tiwa language (TEE-wah), closely related to the Tiwa speech of three other New Mexico pueblos: Picuris, which is about twenty-five miles southeast of Taos, and Isleta and Sandia, which are close to Albuquerque. Here is another source of confusion. Taos and the other Tiwa languages are also related to Tewa (TAY-wah). Tewa is spoken by the pueblos of San Juan, Santa Clara, San Ildefonso, Nambé, Pojoaque, and Tesuque. These are all villages south of Taos in the area around Española and Santa Fe. The problem has been that even knowledgeable persons have written Tewa to refer to the language of Taos, when they should have spelled it Tiwa. It should be added that the people of Jemez Pueblo speak Towa (TOW-wah). Tiwa, Tewa, and Towa all belong to the group of languages known at Tanoan (tah-NO-un). Hopefully, it is not terribly confusing to add that the Indians of other New Mexico pueblos speak languages totally unrelated to Tanoan. The Pueblos of Cochiti, Santo Domingo, San Felipe, Santa Ana, Zia, Laguna, and

Taos Pueblo, ca. 1930, by Forman Hanna.

Acoma, which are either between Santa Fe and Albuquerque or west of Albuquerque, speak Keres (CARE-us). The language of the Indians of Zuni Pueblo in western New Mexico south of Gallup is again separate from all of the above.

It is interesting that languages spoken by the Pueblo Indians are indeed of several groups and quite different from one another. This baffles many people who tend to think that there is "an Indian language." Nothing could be further from the truth. One need only reflect on the complex language situation in Europe: Basque is not related to French, although French is related to English, but English is more closely related to German. None is related to Hungarian. All this does not seem to bother most people, but when it comes to Indian languages, for some reason they are either confused or bored. The myth persists that Indians speak Indian, and "Indian" is often thought of as primitive, guttural, and not complicated grammatically.

Taos is a very beautiful language; it is also a very complex one and extremely difficult to learn. The Taos are very polite people, particularly when communicating with each other. Perhaps there is a relationship between this and the fact that it is impossible to be profane in Taos and very difficult to be obscene. One thing that should startle English speakers is that you cannot directly say "no" in Taos, nor is there a concept of "never." Imagine the effect this would have on English conversation! The ultimate origin of the Taos language and the hundreds of other languages spoken by the American Indians is unknown, although the Indians themselves first came from Asia. Racially they are Asiatic in origin; and if one went back far enough, say 25,000 years, it could be said that their languages are also Asiatic. But no known Asiatic language can be linked with any Indian language spoken today in the United States—and Taos is most definitely not related to Chinese any more than Chinese is related to Japanese!

SOME HISTORICAL NOTES ON THE PUEBLO

Too little is still known of Taos Pueblo to give a completely satisfactory history. This is especially true of the history of the Taos people before the coming of the Spanish. It seems certain that Taos Pueblo was built some time around AD 1350. Precisely when the ancestors of the Taos first entered the valley is impossible to state, although there are numerous Pueblo ruins here and there that are certainly older than Taos Pueblo. Most archaeologists think that the Pueblo

Indians who settled along the Rio Grande migrated from the Four Corners region—the area where the present states of Colorado, New Mexico, Arizona, and Utah meet. The spectacular ruins and cliff

dwellings of that region, such as Mesa Verde, Chaco, and Kayenta, were inhabited by the Anasazi, a word meaning "old ones" in Navajo. A long drought that plagued the area in the late 1200s and other factors may have caused the Anasazi to abandon their great villages and move east to the Rio Grande where the water supply was more dependable. If so, then the Taos and their neighbors are descendants of these "old ones."

Another theory is that the Tanoan-speaking people, including the Taos, were nomadic and roamed somewhere in the north until they moved south into the Rio Grande Valley. Here they encountered the Keres, who we recall do not speak a language related to Tanoan. Perhaps the Keres speakers were migrants from the Four Corners. The Tanoans adopted agriculture and the Pueblo way of life and so came to resemble the "old ones" in the process. It is interesting that the Kiowa language is related to Tanoan. The Kiowa are true Plains Indians now living in Oklahoma. There are many words in Taos, for example, that are the same in Kiowa. Actually, the whole matter is much more complicated than this, but the arguments continue. It will be up to the anthropologists and other

North side of South Pueblo, Taos Pueblo, ca. 1912, by Jesse L Nusbaum.

scientists to finally unravel the matter. The Taos themselves say only that they came from the north.

Taos Pueblo fiesta, ca. 1920, by George L. Beam.

After the Spanish arrived, first with Coronado in 1540 and later with Juan de Oñate to settle the Rio Grande Valley in 1598, the history of Taos Pueblo becomes much clearer. Many fine books have been written on this history, although a number of facts about Taos Pueblo itself are not known. But for the history buff it is not difficult to obtain a good outline of the past. It is important that the Taos people have preserved their way of life for nearly four hundred years in the face of strong pressure by Spaniards and Anglo-Americans. They have adopted many things from these other cultures but have refused to become absorbed by them. They rely very firmly on a cultural base that was laid down centuries ago and remain convinced that, while many good things have come from the Europeans, the Taos have a heritage worth preserving. It is apparent from what one sees at Taos Pueblo today that they have succeeded.

THE COMMUNITY

Perhaps nothing is stronger at Taos Pueblo than a deep feeling of belonging to a community. This communal spirit, expressed in the phrase "We are in one nest," has been one of the most important things that has held the people of Taos together. There are many responsibilities and obligations that every Taos Indian must accept to remain a respected member of the community. For example, both men and women are expected to offer their services when needed. These are collectively known as "community duties." They range from helping to clean out irrigation ditches in the spring, to serving in the native government, to correctly performing religious ritual, to preparing food for ceremonial occasions. Ideally, one should be very cooperative, which is not to say that Taos people do not quarrel among themselves at times—there are a number of very strong-willed people at the Pueblo. That is true today just as it was in the past, but one should never allow one's own desires to be destructive of community interests.

In the Council, the principal governing body of the Pueblo, this ideal of cooperation is expressed by the statement, "Let us move evenly together." Although more will be said about the governing structure of the Pueblo, it is important to know that an individual should always bow to the will of the whole, and the whole must be taken very literally. Unlike the American concept of the will of the majority, the Pueblo belief in the strength of everyone moving unanimously is something very difficult to achieve. It has caused serious problems from time to time, but it has also been a strong force that has prevented Taos from breaking apart.

THE FAMILY

At the root of this communal spirit and certainly one of the strongest institutions at Taos is the family. A Taos family is organized in much the same way as an Anglo-American family, though in many instances it is bigger and more closely knit. The Taos have a bilateral kinship system: descent on both the father's and mother's sides of the family is equally recognized. This is the same system that prevails in American families. Since at Taos both sides are important, this means that you consider a very large number of people to belong to your family. You treat them and expect them to treat you as family members. The result is that you are related to many people and are expected to help and be helped by a great many more relatives than most American families of today. Since the majority of these relatives live nearby rather than hundreds of miles away, it is easy to see how close many Taos families actually are. This doesn't mean you like all your relatives any more than would be true elsewhere, but again you are supposed to be cooperative and try to submerge your feelings for the good of all. Also important at Taos is a very strong respect for the aged. Even if you disagree with their advice, you should have the courtesy to consult with your elders about any important matter.

In the majority of cases at Taos, each primary family lives in a separate dwelling—that is, at marriage the young couple sets up a residence of their own for themselves and the children that hopefully will be born. But members of your own family and that of your wife's or husband's are always near. This has been very important in

South side of South Pueblo, Taos Pueblo, ca. 1912, by Jesse L Nusbaum.

raising children. As young adults have had to go out of the Pueblo and into the wage-earning world, older relatives, particularly grand-parents, have been available to take care of the children. Naturally this meant that they taught these youngest Taos Indians what they felt was important in life. Values and ways of doing things that they cherished were thereby handed down and tended to protect the integrity of Taos culture. So yet another generation of Taos Indians loyal to their heritage was nurtured.

POPULATION

It was mentioned at the beginning that there were approximately 1,500 Taos Indians living at the Pueblo today. There were actually a little fewer than 2,000 persons recorded on the tribal rolls in 1991. The Taos population has grown dramatically in the past few decades and especially since the Second World War. In 1942, for example, there were only 830 Taos on the rolls. This increase has had important effects at the Pueblo. As the population grew, more and more Taos Indians, particularly young adults, left to seek employment, most often in the cities. Some 500 are scattered across the country with many in the Western cities of Albuquerque,

Denver, Phoenix, and Los Angeles. While this has tended to split up a number of families, many remain intact and the old ways continue. Often individuals leave for a relatively short time (a few years) and then return, so there is a rather constant fluctuation of the population. If possible, many come home for major feast days, at Christmas, and on vacation. Since enough have stayed permanently at the Pueblo, no serious threat to the continuation of Taos culture has occurred.

DRESS AND ORNAMENTATION

Before the arrival of Europeans, the Taos people dressed primarily in skin clothing: buckskin shirts and leggings for the men and dresses for the women. All wore hard-soled moccasins. Of course, all these items of dress were handmade by the people from animals they hunted. The mountains were well stocked with deer, and the Taos went frequently to the plains to the east to hunt buffalo. Taos Valley is too high and the growing season too short for cotton, so the Taos traded for woven cotton goods with the Indians to the south. Cotton was domesticated independently in the New World by the

Taos woman in traditional dress with a pot traded in from elsewhere.

American Indians. The Spanish brought sheep with them into New Mexico, so eventually woolen goods were also available. The Spanish also introduced cowhide. Taos dress styles have thus changed through the centuries.

Today store-bought clothing is worn, so that in most respects the Taos dress much like everyone else in the country, particularly like other rural Western people. There are a few important differences that can be observed, however. Older Taos men tend to imitate the dress styles of former times. They usually wear moccasins or shoes with the heels removed to simulate the moccasin style. They rarely wear hats and will often cut out the seat of store-bought pants to resemble the skin leggings of the past. A breech clout is worn and a cloth is wrapped around the hips to cover themselves. They wear their hair long and plaited in two braids that begin behind the ears and fall forward on the chest. Most importantly, they are rarely seen without the blanket.

The blanket, which has been the cause of much discussion by those who visit Taos Pueblo, serves a number of purposes. Obviously, it is a source of warmth in the winter, but people wonder why it is also worn in the summer. Actually, it rarely gets so hot in Taos that the blanket is truly uncomfortable. In summer, the men lower the blanket and wrap it securely around their waist and hips. It can also be folded and wrapped bulkily around the head, providing a turban-like hat which acts as an effective sun shade. Most often this is done when working in the fields. People of North Africa and the Middle East, where it gets much hotter, wrap themselves in similar ways. There, such clothing styles definitely act as protection against the penetrating rays of the sun; but the most important reason is a cultural one, just as it is at Taos. It is both a custom and a symbol of being a Taos Indian. It is interesting that none of the other Pueblo Indians, except the Picuris, ever wore the blanket in this manner, which raises the question of where this custom originated. Most probably it was adopted from the southern Plains Indians of Oklahoma. The Taos have very close ties with many of these tribes. Photographs taken before the turn of the twentieth century show Cheyenne and Arapaho, among others, wearing the blanket in the same manner as the Taos do today. Precisely when it was adopted at Taos is not known, but probably around 1890.

Adult women at Taos, except for ceremonial occasions, do not maintain as many customs of dress as the men. The women do

prefer low or flat shoes. For one thing, walking around in high heels at the Pueblo is hardly practical. But it is only when they are costumed for dances, such as the Corn Dances in summer, that you can observe the older style of dress. While dresses worn on these occasions are made of commercial cloth, they are cut in traditional fashion to leave one shoulder bare and are belted at the waist with a wide sash. The costume is not complete without the folded white doeskin boots owned by every adult woman. Often they were made and presented to a bride by the groom at the time of their wedding. Older Taos women will sometimes wear them today on other than ceremonial occasions. They also often wear their hair in a chignon, the hair drawn to the back of the head and wrapped in a double vertical bun secured with woolen yarn. The most distinctive item of dress is the shawl. Older adult women hardly ever go anywhere, summer or winter, without one. Cotton or wool, it is de rigueur, just as the blanket is for men.

It is not customary for the Taos to wear a great deal of jewelry and other ornamentation, except on special occasions. However, this depends largely on the individual. Southwestern Indian jewelry in

Taos Pueblo, New Mexico, ca. 1930, by Forman Hanna.

all its variety is owned by the Taos, just as it is by both the Spanish- and Anglo-Americans. The Taos do not load themselves down with silver and turquoise as do the Navajo because it is not considered proper to display one's wealth and good fortune. For the Navajo it is important to do so. They wear their jewelry for different and equally valid cultural reasons.

ECONOMICS

Before the coming of the Spanish and for a considerable period after that, the Indians of Taos Pueblo were largely self-sufficient. Their land was rich and well-watered. Most years saw an abundant harvest. In addition to agriculture, the Taos hunted game animals and birds. They carried on a certain amount of trade with other Indian tribes, and they still do. But prior to the coming of the Anglo-Americans in the nineteenth century, the economy was principally one of barter. Today it is a strictly cash economy. Wage work has replaced farming as a primary means of making a living. There are a few who still depend on agriculture and livestock, and some families plant gardens and raise pigs and chickens. But these products are almost entirely consumed by the families who maintain them.

Many people question why agriculture does not remain the primary source of support for the Taos. There are two very obvious and logical reasons: First, as a result of the population increase and through equal inheritance patterns, the land has become reduced to smaller and smaller plots which are insufficient for meaningful agricultural production. Second, agriculture, to be profitable today, requires considerable capital and a highly mechanized operation. This is impossible for most Indians to achieve. This area of northern New Mexico is one of the most economically depressed regions in the country. In spite of the fact that many Indians are more affluent than they were in the past, unemployment is very high. There are simply not enough jobs in the Taos area for the people who could fill them. This is another major reason for the significant number of Taos Indians who have left to find employment elsewhere.

Many believe that the federal government supports Indian people. Strictly speaking, this is false. The government does provide health and educational facilities for Indians living on reservations, such as the Taos. And reservation land is not taxed. But Indians are subject to the same income and other taxes as every other U.S. citizen, and they must pay the same price for all goods and services. Of considerable importance to the Taos in recent years have been the various forms of welfare assistance, social security payments, and pensions. These programs do not differ from similar ones available to other people in the country, particularly those who are living at a virtual level of poverty. They have become tremendously helpful to the many aged persons at the Pueblo and have relieved the younger generations by their complete support.

It is truly remarkable in many instances how the Indians have survived economically, since the annual per capita income is often only a few hundred dollars, so low as to make the government's poverty-level figures absolutely absurd when applied to their situation. No one starves at the Pueblo. Again, this is due in part to the close family ties. Sharing resources, particularly food, is a time-honored Indian custom and tends to distribute what excess there is. Some Indians are certainly better off than others, but very few can meet the standards accepted as normal by the majority of middle-class Americans. The Taos are not overly impressed by material goods; in fact, it is not a cultural value to try to amass wealth. It is certainly in bad taste to make any open display of one's good fortune.

The Taos Indians were favorite subjects of photographers in the past as well as today.

GOVERNMENT

The Taos have maintained a very interesting form of government. The principal governing body of the Pueblo is the Council, which is made up of the most important religious leaders representing the six Taos kivas and the top secular officers who have served or are serving as Governor, Lieutenant Governor, War Chief, and Assistant War Chief. The Council numbers around fifty men. Women do not hold positions in Taos government. In order to be elected by the Council to one of the four important secular offices, a man must have been initiated into the kiva religious system; therefore, Taos government has been described as a theocracy.

While the Council must decide on all truly important issues that face the Pueblo, the secular officers are in charge of day-to-day matters that affect the community. The secular staff changes each year and is annually elected and installed on January 1. The Governor and his staff concern themselves with everything that occurs inside the village, while the War Chief and his staff see to anything external to the village, but on reservation land. For example, it is the War Chief's responsibility to patrol the mountainous areas for instances of trespass or forest fire. In recent years this division of labor has tipped somewhat in favor of the Governor, who has become more important than the War Chief. The money collected from visitors through parking and photographic fees, which is a primary source of income for the community, is the responsibility of the Governor. Most often he will be the one contacted by federal or state agencies should anything arise that concerns the tribe. In turn, the matter, if serious enough, must go before the Council.

It was mentioned previously that a unanimous decision by the Council is highly desirable. At least general agreement is usually sought. It is on this basis that Taos government has been described as exceedingly democratic. From a strictly American perspective, however, this is not literally true, since the members of the Council are not the elected representatives of all the people. Nevertheless, it is a system that has operated at Taos for untold generations, and the Council is recognized by the United States government as the legitimate governing body of the Pueblo. Until the Taos themselves decide to change it, it will undoubtedly continue.

RELIGION AND THE CEREMONIAL CALENDAR

Though the Taos religion is most important to the continuance of their traditional culture, the Taos do not want their religion revealed to outsiders. They feel that strength is maintained by carefully guarding the nature of their religious ritual and performance. Part of this determination not to reveal the operation of the kiva-based religion is due to the fact that the Taos were persecuted in the early days of Spanish occupation for practicing their aboriginal rites. Subsequent to the Anglo-American takeover, the Taos felt again the sting of religious persecution, particularly in the early decades of the twentieth century.

It is known that Taos religion is based on a belief in the oneness of all living things. Religious ritual is aimed at protecting the delicate balance of the relationship between man and nature. Each kiva at Taos has its own special role to perform in this overall task, but to say anything beyond this would be offensive to the Taos people. What occurs in the kivas and at the many sacred "shrines" in the mountains behind the Pueblo is not the business of outsiders. Until such time as the Taos decide it is necessary to record their religion for the future, it is a subject best not approached. Unfortunately,

Chifonete pole, Feast of San Geronimo, 1902, by H. S. Poley.

many outsiders have engaged in idle speculation, some of it totally misleading and often absolutely false. At times this has been very harmful to the community and completely unwarranted in a country which professes freedom of religious worship.

The Taos generously permit outsiders to witness the public portions of certain ceremonies, so it is possible to list the important dances that are performed each year. They in turn partially reflect the ceremonial calendar of Taos religion. You are fortunate if your visit to the Pueblo coincides with one of these remarkable performances.

Although the Taos perform other dances at various times of the year, they are not regularly scheduled on particular dates, so it is necessary to inquire whether a dance will be held. But it is obvious from our list that the Taos have organized the sequence of dances in accordance with the Catholic calendar. This is the result of the long-standing influence of Catholicism at Taos. However, with the exception of the procession from the church on Christmas Eve when the statue of the Virgin is carried around the village and the performance of the Matachines—a dance of Spanish and Mexican origin—all ceremonies are Indian in nature.

TAOS PUEBLO CALENDAR OF DANCES

January 1   Turtle Dance

January 6   Buffalo or Deer Dance

May 3   Feast of Santa Cruz: foot race and Corn Dance

June 13   Feast of San Antonio: Corn Dance

June 24   Feast of San Juan: Corn Dance

July 25   Feast of Santa Ana: Corn Dance

July 26   Feast of Santiago: Corn Dance

September 29 and 30   Feast of San Geronimo: Sunset Dance, foot
   race, pole climbing, annual Taos Fair

Christmas Eve   Procession

Christmas Day   Deer Dance or Matachines

The "animal dances" in winter, such as the Turtle, Buffalo, and Deer, are generally regarded by those who have seen them to be the most beautiful that the Taos perform. This may be due to the great importance the Taos placed formerly on hunting such animals as deer and buffalo. The so-called Corn Dances in summer are actually

OVERLEAF: *Foot races on major feast day, San Geronimo, September 30, 1893,* by George E. Stewart.

intended for the success of agricultural endeavors. Women participate more in these dances than in the animal dances of winter, with the exception of the Deer Dance. The Turtle and Buffalo dances are strictly male performances.

The Feast of San Geronimo, the patron saint of Taos, is a two-day celebration that marks the close of the harvest season. In the late 1700s and early 1800s Taos was the site of annual trade fairs that attracted hundreds of Indians from other tribes and many other persons who came to trade and barter goods. San Geronimo is reflective of this even today. Also on San Geronimo, the Black Eyes religious society performs.

They are often referred to in English as the Clowns (Chifonete) because of their amusing antics, although their behavior is actually of a serious nature. They climb a very tall pole erected in the village on the north side not too far from the church. At the top of the pole, the freshly killed carcass of a sheep and bundles of food have been fastened. It is the duty of the pole climber to bring these down, whereupon they are distributed among the Black Eyes who have participated.

Early on the morning of September 30 there is a foot race on the track that runs east and west between the north-side houses and the drying racks. A good deal of misunderstanding has been generated about the meaning of these races. It is often thought they are an example of spirited competition, as one would expect in a competitive sport such as track. Rather, they are religious in nature and are aimed at the maintenance of physical well-being, not only for the racers but for the community as a whole. Each participant should do his best. It is less important who wins, and it is not a race that pits the north-side people against the south-side. It is certain that most who have the opportunity to see these dances and other activities feel they have gained considerable insight into the strength and integrity of Taos culture.

THE FUTURE

For a long time many people in this country firmly believed that the Indians and their way of life would fade from the scene. Some were even so rash as to predict how long it would take. In the case of Taos, one writer stated in 1936 that it would probably be only about fifty years before the culture of the Taos Indians disintegrated and the people were absorbed into the mythical melting pot of the United States. This has not happened, nor is there any firm indication that it will in the foreseeable future. All over the country Indian people have survived the incredible onslaught of programs aimed at their assimilation into the mainstream of American life. There are signs that in many respects their determination to be Indian is stronger now than during some periods of the past. They have held on tenaciously to a philosophy and way of life that they believe is in many ways more satisfactory than what they see in the outside world. It is futile to make predictions about the extinction of Taos culture.

There have been many deep changes in the culture since the arrival of the Europeans. Undoubtedly other changes will yet occur. Many changes, however, are of a superficial nature—to drive a pickup truck instead of a wagon and team of horses does not mean that the driver is any less "Indian." Electricity has been permitted on many parts of the reservation, although not in the old village itself. More and more Taos Indians are seeking college and university educations. Many are acquiring the technical skills to compete in the world beyond the Pueblo, but time-honored values and attitudes that are intrinsically Indian remain. Importantly, many of the young people are experiencing a renewed commitment to the traditions of their ancestors. There is no point in being brutally realistic about the many problems that the Taos will face in the future. It is even of less benefit to wax romantic over an imaginary illustrious past that in some ways never existed.

The Taos have demonstrated tremendous strength in their determination to preserve what they feel is culturally important. Perhaps no more important indication of that strength was evident than on December 15, 1970, when the news reached the Pueblo that the president had signed into law the bill returning Blue Lake and the surrounding sacred lands to their reservation. For sixty-four years the Taos had battled the massive machinery of the federal government. The fight in the House of Representatives and then in the Senate demonstrated the unwillingness of many politicians to listen to the just plea of a small group of American Indians. The Taos were supported by many people outside the Pueblo, but it was their own steadfast conviction that finally won the battle. It was in many ways a symbol of the strength of their heritage. Taos culture will continue for as long as the people want it to, regardless of the tolerance or intolerance of the wider culture that surrounds them. Their culture is not only of the past. It is also of the present and future.

‖ ADDITIONAL READINGS ‖

Bahti, Mark. *Pueblo Stories and Storytellers*. Tucson, AZ: Rio Nuevo Publishers, 1996.

Bodine, John J. "Taos Pueblo" in *Handbook of North American Indians*, Vol. 9. Alfonso Ortiz, ed. Washington, DC: Smithsonian Institution, 1997.

Gibson, Daniel. *Pueblos of the Rio Grande: A Visitor's Guide*. Tucson, AZ: Rio Nuevo Publishers, 2002.

Gordon-McCutchan, R. C. *The Taos Indians and the Battle for Blue Lake*. Santa Fe, NM: Red Crane Books, 1991.

Lowry, Joe Dan, and Joe P. Lowry. *Turquoise Unearthed: An Illustrated Guide*. Tucson, AZ: Rio Nuevo Publishers, 2002.

Sando, Joe S. *Pueblo Nations: Eight Centuries of Pueblo Indian History*. Santa Fe, NM: Clear Light Publishers, 1992.

Trimble, Stephen. *The People: Indians of the American Southwest*. Santa Fe, NM: School of American Research, 1993.

Waters, Frank. *The Man Who Killed the Deer*. Athens, GA: Swallow Press, 1984.